DEMON DIARY

Translator - Lauren Na
English Adaptation - Kelly Sue DeConnick
Retouch and Lettering - Christina R. Siri
Cover Layout - Aaron Suhr
Graphic Designer - Deron Bennett

Editor - Rob Tokar
Managing Editor - Jill Freshney
Production Coordinator - Antonio DePietro
Production Managers - Jennifer Miller & Mutsumi Miyazaki
Art Director - Matt Alford
Editorial Director - Jeremy Ross
VP of Production - Ron Klamert
President & C.O.O. - John Parker
Publisher & C.E.O. - Stuart Levy

Email: editor@TOKYOPOP.com
Come visit us online at www.TOKYOPOP.com

A  Manga

TOKYOPOP Inc.
5900 Wilshire Blvd. Suite 2000
Los Angeles, CA 90036

Demon Diary Vol. 5

ISBN: 1-59182-430-3

First TOKYOPOP printing: January 2004

10 9 8 7 6 5 4 3 2

Printed in the USA

DEMON DIARY

Art by Kara
Story by Lee Yun Hee

Volume 5

Los Angeles • Tokyo • London

Who's Who In Demon Diary

An orphan, Raenef had to join thieves at an early age in order to survive. Among the thieves, Raenef's kind, gentle, and somewhat ditzy nature made him stand out. Approached by Eclipse, Raenef was eager for a change from his life of stealing to eat. Unfortunately, Raenef's cheerful and kind-hearted qualities are even less desirable in a demon lord than they are in a thief. Though a poor student and a regular source of embarrassment for Eclipse, Raenef desperately wants to become the greatest demon lord ever.

Raenef

Eclipse

Eclipse is a demon of the highest order with an impressive resume. When the fourth Demon Lord Raenef died without designating an heir, Eclipse was charged with finding and mentoring Raenef the Fifth. Tall, dark, and mysterious, Eclipse is a wise and noble demon and his new pupil's ineptitude is a blow to Eclipse's prestige in the Demon Courts. Despite their differences, Eclipse finds himself strangely drawn to Raenef.

Sensing powerful magic coming from Raenef's castle, the human knight Erutis intended to build her reputation by slaying the demon lord within. At first, she found it hard to take Raenef seriously but, after the demon lord-in-training shattered her sword, Erutis soon found herself outmatched. To save her own life, she convinced Raenef to take her on as his henchman rather than killing her. Since then, they have become close friends.

Erutis

The sole survivor of a demonic attack on his hometown, Chris was rescued and adopted by Hejem, High Cleric of the nearby Temple of Rased. As Hejem's disciple, Chris is destined to be the temple's next High Cleric. Though the god Rased suppressed Chris' memories of the traumatic attack, Chris has retained an intense hatred of demons. Against Hejem's wishes, Chris created a Demon Summoning sign and captured Raenef. The scuffle between the Demon Lord-in-training and the future High Cleric was brief and, as an apology (and to teach Chris humility), Hejem sent Chris to live with Raenef for a short time. Despite himself, Chris has developed a friendship with Raenef.

Chris

A female demon, Meruhesae is also a powerful seer. When Eclipse was assigned to locate Raenef the Fifth, it was Meruhesae who pointed the demon in the right direction.

Meruhesae

THE STORY SO FAR
You will seek the 5th Raenef.
Demon Lord Raenef the Fourth is dead. Usually, a Demon Lord selects an heir and grooms him or her for the new role but, if tragedy should befall the demon lord before an heir has been appointed, other measures must be taken. In every generation, there is one among the mortals who bears the name of a demon lord...and the one who bears that name is the deceased demon lord's successor.
Enter Raenef, an orphaned street urchin and, unbeknownst to him, the heir to demon royalty. Unfortunately, with a personality that is incredibly sweet, nice and friendly, Raenef couldn't be further from demon lord material. Assigned by the gods to be Raenef's tutor, Eclipse is a wise and noble demon faced with the seemingly impossible task of molding Raenef into a proper demon lord.
The gods agree, of all demons...
...you, who have served so many so well, are best suited to locate the demon lord who already exists in the world.

What?!
You? You're the demon lord?!
A demon lord's life is not without peril, however, and Raenef has already faced several attacks by those bent on destroying his kind. However, due to Raenef's lovable nature, two of his attackers (a human knight known as Erutis and the future High Cleric to the Temple of Rased named Chris) now live in Raenef's castle as his companions.
After repeatedly failing in his quest to become a proper demon lord, Raenef has finally made good...by becoming bad. The usually pleasant, cute and cuddly Raenef has become dark, frightening and haughty--in other words, a typically terrible demon lord. Concerned by Raenef's sudden change, Erutis, Chris, and Eclipse hunt for the cause of Raenef's transformation...
Game over, kid...

We'll start from the beginning.

So, this is the last place he was before his personality changed, right?

Yes, there must be something here that disturbed Master Raenef.

We're not going to find anything in here...

Except **dust**.

Humph, it's not like his whole personality would change if he didn't like the wallpaper.

Why is there a mortal in a demon lord's castle?

Erutis, you have found it.

Yiiiiiiiipess!

Th-th-the b-book! The b-book is talking!
Books do not talk--and books DO NOT LEVITATE!!

pleasedon'tbeaghost pleasedon'tbeaghost
(Erutis is not crazy about ghosts.)

철퍼덕

That book is a low-ranking demon created by Demon Lord Raenef IV, probably as a storage vessel.

A low-ranking demon?

A book?

Remarkably unfazed -.-;;

Humph! "Low-ranking demon" hardly does me justice. Allow me to introduce myself.

I am Yohaim Alexis Fernando Reinhardt Wyferon Versailles de Granvirias.

You may call me "Granvirias," for short.

Huh.

It talks, it floats, it has a name...

Naming things was one of Demon Lord Raenef IV's hobbies.

That is one of the last vestiges of his handiwork.

You're a lot smarter than you look, hotshot.
That's right, I changed him into a true demon lord. You're welcome.
Tell me, book--
휙
I told you, my name is Granvir--
Book! Tell me...
How can we return Master Raenef to his natural state?

Why would you want to do that?
He finally acts like a demon lord.

......

You should be pleased. Explain yourself!
I advise you to reconsider your tone...
...book.

The current Master Raenef is not his true self.
All beings must be true to themselves above all else...
Even--and especially--a demon lord such as Master Raenef.
The idea that a measly creature such as yourself has dared alter his character...
...**that** is something that I, as his servant, cannot accept.

How can it be undone?

Hey--

Hey, you, young man--

Young man...?
It's talking to you.

YOUNG MAN YOUNG MA
YOUNG MAN YOUNG MA
YOUNG MAN YOUNG MA
YOUNG MAN YOUNG MA
YOUNG MAN YOUNG MA
YOUNG MAN YOUNG MA
YOUNG MAN YOUNG MA
YOUNG MAN YOUNG M
YOUNG MAN YOUNG MA
YOUNG MA OUNG MA
YOUNG NG MA
YOUNG IG MA
YOUNG NG MA
YOUNG NG MA
YOUNG G MA
YOUNG NG MA

C'mere, book!!

Well!
I never--!!
In all my--
SWORDSMAN'S REDECORATING.
If one page is damaged, you will be held responsible!
You, young man, could stand--
What is wrong with you, young man?
When I was your age, young men showed respect!

Let go of me! I'm gonna make confetti out of that book!!

Calm down! Quit it!

It's not the book's fault...

That you look like a boy!

IMBECILES.

What?!!!

You know you look like a boy.

Ignore them.

So, how can Master Raenef be restored?

Well, it's a little tricky.
Hey! Young m--
Erutis.
Yeah, you! Come here and open me up to page 182.

......
A frilly pink dress...and ribbons.
And this has to be performed by--

Eclipse?
Imagining
Awake, Fair Prince!! ♥
PFFTT
푸하하하
Bwa ha ha ha!!
I had you going there for a minute, didn't I?

Pink! Frilly! Dress! Ha ha ha ha ha! I gotcha, all right.

Hee hee hee! Really, I kill me.

Eclipse's black aura
I hereby summon the shadows of all true evil...
The darkest energies of this world...

Erutis, help me!!
Eclipse, calm down!
Wha-- huh?!!
Armageddon!
A most powerful dark magic.

Now that's just mean.

If I can't move my pages, I can't do anything.

fuss fuss π.π

Be grateful I don't believe in burning books.

What? I was just joking! Sheesh.

Even as I sit here, I'm pondering the destruction of the human world, and the rebirth of a new world in my image.

A world fit for me.

Oblivious
Seriously, how do we change Raenef back? And no garbage--
--if I hadn't intervened, Eclipse would have torched you and half the castle.
Not a good idea to kid Eclipse.

Uh... well...
힐끔

I don't know...I mean, I don't think you can.
If I tell, I'm dead.

Master Raenef cannot be unenchanted?
He is still Master Raenef and it is true that he is now a proper demon lord.
However...
...those eyes...

It is not... fitting.
They are so cold.
Eclipse.

.....!
Hello?
!!

Hey, you!
You're--!!

끼이이
Creeek
번쩍
Startled

Show yourself!!

Er...it's me, sire.
I've been commanded to return you to your original state, master.
HA!
Ha ha ha!
M-Master Raenef?
Very funny.
My original state, eh?

How dare you?!
Did you think I would quietly submit to regression?
파직
You've forgotten your place, demon.
If you're that eager to die, then I shall oblige you.
파지직
Eeep!!
H-Help!

Your anger is misdirected, child.
He was merely obeying my orders...

...Demon Lord Raenef V.

How is it possible for you to be here?
But-- how...?
My poor child...

What began with me 150 years ago...
...is now visited upon you.
.....
I don't understand.
Didn't you die?

It is not yet time for your awakening.
......
No, don't--!
!!

Uh...you called?

You should not have used the child...

For your entertainment.

Oh yeah, that...uh...I'm-I'm sorry?!!
The 5th Master Raenef wanted to become a true Demon Lord, so I...I helped--
Vanish!
!!

!!

Ahhhhh! M-Master Raenef!

Forgive me!!

Insignificant fool.

Aw, man...
I sure wish Raenef would snap out of it.
If he doesn't, I'll have no choice but to rise up against the evil Demon Lord and--
Hey, cut it out.
That was only funny the first three or four times you said it.
Can't quite reach!
Oh yeah, it's not like I'm the hero or anything. This is Demon Diary, not Cleric Diary. I'm nobody special!
He's definitely losing it.

Yawn
!!
For some reason, I'm still sleepy.
Heh heh!
Good morning, everyone!

......
?
Why are you all looking at me like that?
Did something happen?
R-Raenef?
He looks like himself, doesn't he?
I-I think so.
Perhaps the enchantment was temporary? Come to think of it, I have not seen that book of late...
It's... it's nothing.
?

Okay. So...
Shouldn't we get ready to go to the demon world?

I'll do my best not to embarrass you this time.

Ready?
For what?
Remember, there's that meeting we have to attend.

Raenef, you're not going to that meeting.
Don't you remember?

Huh?
What? Really?
Why can't I remember?
Did I say I wasn't going?
How strange...

What's going on? Oh, I have to remember or they might fire me as the protagonist!
......

You do not...
Remember anything?

No!

Welcome back, Raenef.

Woe is me!
He's back to himself, all right.
......

Hey, Eclipse. Feel better?
!

Master Raenef is Master Raenef...
...regardless of his relative charms.

Oh, really?
씨익
......

Then what was with that smile a minute ago?
If I didn't know better, I'd say that you were downright jovial.

Nonsense!
Jovial? What are you, a poet?
He has no idea that he smiled.

Heh!

You're very lucky, Raenef. You may be a moron most of the time, but you sure are loved!

Just a moment ago, Eclipse was gazing at you with such sincere affection--

All right, all right! I'll write a poem!

Ooofah.

There's nothing to be ashamed of, Eclipse. What? Are you embarrassed?

Ouch!

What are you two fighting about?

You guys...?

This...is the castle of a demon lord?

Yeow--

Khe-khlang

Flame Flame

Looks more like a zoo.

cK

Somehow...

...I've lost my way AGAIN.
This is the same corridor as a moment ago! How many times is that?

Who needs a castle this big?!

Are you lost again?
What are you doing?
Oh, Raenef!
!
Hoo hoo hoo! Lost? I was just having my prayer time in solace.
Me, lost? Not a chance.
?
You were praying by going around and around in circles?
You passed through here three times.
Watched from the very beginning
!!
You were watching me all that time and didn't even bother to help me?!!
Huh? Help you? With what?

I thought you were praying...?

......

You know, you really are a demon lord--I can definitely sense your powers.

I can't remember anything that happened.
You know, once you've become a bloodthirsty demon lord...
후후후후
...I will annihilate you. And my name will be renowned all over the world!
음하하하
Chris is so creepy sometimes.
This is the first time I've been to this area.
Really?

What's this room?
This was the room of the former Demon Lord Raenef.

Hm.

The demon lord before dimwit here was supposedly a REAL demon lord! A real bloodthirsty villain, a womanizer hunting for blood in the night.

You're thinking of a vampire, not a demon lord.

Let's look inside.

Wow. It's pretty bleak.

Look!
It's a portrait.

Huh. I guess I wasn't expecting him to be so good-looking.
I've never seen him before.

The more powerful the demon lord, the longer he lives...
So this demon lord must have been pretty weak.
!

You became the demon lord because he died, right?

?

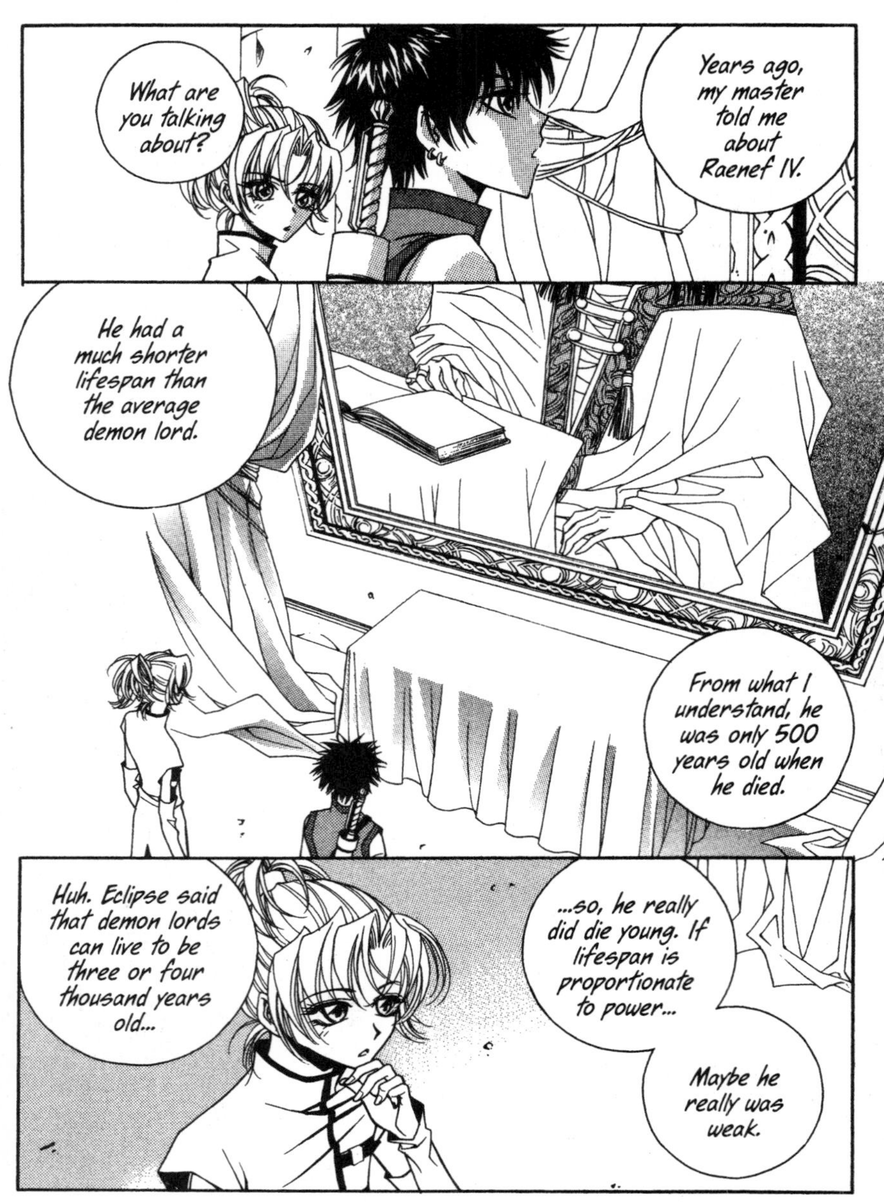
Years ago, my master told me about Raenef IV.
What are you talking about?
He had a much shorter lifespan than the average demon lord.
From what I understand, he was only 500 years old when he died.
...so, he really did die young. If lifespan is proportionate to power...
Maybe he really was weak.
Huh. Eclipse said that demon lords can live to be three or four thousand years old...

Raenef IV was not weak.
Eclipse.
I have been looking for you. I did not expect to find you here.
I wonder if there was another reason...

If it wasn't weakness ...
Eclipse! ♡
꺄 아
...then why did he die so young?
......
In the history of the Raenef Demon Lords--indeed in the history of all Demon Lords--Raenef IV was the most powerful.

Then what happened to him?

He didn't die of natural causes, did he?

Do you want to know?
Yes, please!
쫑긋
쫑긋

Puppy dog eyes...?
Arf! Arf!

So he really was weak.
If one compared Demon Lord Raenef IV to the others, one could say that he possessed less magic, naturally.
Tense Atmosphere!
What? You wanna step outside?
Talking tough, but scared.
However, he discovered a way to magnify his powers.

He learned incantations.
Demon lords normally use their magic without incantations. By using them, Raenef IV was able to get exponentially more powerful results from what little power he possessed.
And his incantations were only effective when recited by him.
I thought that any demon lord could memorize an incantation?

He understood them...
And he became obsessed with their use.
Though the powers of demon lords may seem similar, they have differing traits.
The incantations that the former Raenef Demon Lord wrote could only be used by him.
For the numerous incantations that he developed, he was renowned throughout demonkind as their mightiest.
Huh--he must've been smart.
You haven't told us why he died so young.

150 years ago...
During the Hangma War, the former Demon Lord Raenef killed legions of heaven's creatures with his mighty power.
Do you recall our lessons about the Hangma War?
The war between the demons and heaven's creatures?
No other demon lord matched his might.
The price of this power was the shortening of his life.

Wait a minute!
It was a fight against heaven's creatures and not the gods?
You would know them as gods, Chris.
Mortals refer to heaven's creatures as "gods."
What? I've never heard that before.
It's true. The real gods are way up above and they just observe what happens to us down here.
I saw them once with my very own eyes.
Because the creatures of heaven came down and helped the mortals...
The mortals began to call them "gods" and erected shrines to them.
I see you have been paying attention!
Your reading comprehension is much improved, as well.
Thank you!
......

The battle between the clerics and the demons was just one small part...
...of the war between the creatures of heaven and the demons.
Perhaps because they feared Demon Lord Raenef the most...
The creatures of heaven sacrificed their own lives...
...in order to curse him with an incantation.

What kind of curse?

It is not known.

However, I assure you that the early demise of Demon Lord Raenef IV...
Is related to that curse.

So...
He was cursed to death?

Well, at least he didn't die young because he was weak.

Well, he wasn't strong enough to resist the curse, was he?
Argh!
("Argh" is a witty retort for Raenef.)

파지직
Two sides of the same coin.

The former Demon Lord Raenef understood the details of his curse...
But he never revealed them to anyone.

So, what do we know about the curse?
Jinx.

It is getting late. It's time for you to turn in.

This night, clouds obscure the sky.
The demon lord meeting was a waste of time.
We learned nothing.
And my second sight...
Remains too cloudy to be of use.

A demon lord's power is passed to his heir through his name.

That is what makes demon lord names unique.

I am impressed, Meruhesae.
You obviously have not wasted your many years sitting about.
Very good!
!
You and the others, your curiosity must be killing you.
The fact that the five eldest demons called a meeting is remarkable in itself.
If you're that curious, ask. Should I be so inclined, I'll answer.

Why so quiet all of a sudden?
......
All right. Tell me what happened to you.

150 years ago, during the Hangma War...
...what happened between you and the creatures of heaven?

So...much blood...
Drip drip...

We cannot last much longer.
His power is equaled only by his cruelty.
How doest a single demon generate such power?
Our final option...
...is the sacrificial curse incantation.

Vile demon lord!
We give up our lives!!
To bring down your power!!
?!

투둑
My lord, is something the matter?
......
It's nothing, Eclipse. You may go now.

타ㅇ
......
ZZHING!
Where time stands still, where past and future collide...
...where the sea of time has gathered, storing mysteries in the tide. There gather up in droplets, your wisdom as a rain. Everything I ask of you, I compel you to explain.

Annihilation of the Name.
Ha! I should have guessed that would be the curse of the creatures of heaven.

Those parasites!!
I will destroy them.
Annihilation of the Name!!
Our names are passed from generation to generation, connected to our powers.
Eradicate a demon lord's name...

B-But...
...you must have found a solution...?
Why didn't you destroy heaven's remaining creatures...
!!
...when you had the chance?
...and you effectively erase his future.

I felt it more prudent...
...to conserve my energy...
And focus on combatting the curse.
......

Why do you tell me this now?

I've no doubt you want something from me.

...demon lords do not interfere.

Consider this a warning.

No matter what happens...?

There was something else.
There was something else he chose not to tell me.
One million twenty-one.
One million twenty-two.

드르렁

!

Zzzz.

Poke poke
Hey, sleepy. Wake up.
Your snoring is shaking the ground.
And it's already noon.

Yawn...I'm so sleepy.
How many strokes have you practiced?

......

I forgot.
Start over.
Start over?!

One.
Two. Three.
Zzzzz

Chris?
Um, you look kind of dorky. What few fans you have are going to give up on you.
What are you talking about?! I'm practicing swords-manship!!
You want me to stab you with my stick?!
Why would you use a sword when you're a cleric?
I'll become a Magic Wielding Swordsman!!
I'll be able to use my magic and a sword too.
Sorry, but clerics who use weapons aren't called 'Magic Wielding Swordsmen'-- they're monks. And they really do use sticks.

Cleric: Monk
Level: 2
Weapon: staff (a stick)
Specialty: Clerics usually restrict their abilities to memorizing sacred incantations. However, there are some clerics who use martial arts. These clerics are generally referred to as Monks.

Gasp!
What about me? I'm a demon lord. Demons aren't so bad.
Do you hate me, Chris?
You don't act like a demon lord and...and...
Well... you're different.
Huh?
Huh?

I don't hate you.
You're...
You're my friend, okay?
Heh! So all that talk about destroying me was just talk?
Not so fast, I'm still a cleric!!
One day, we may become enemies!

Should you become an evil demon lord...
...I will fight you.
Even if you are my friend.
Okay!
I consider you my friend too, so I'll make sure to be a kind demon lord.
What? Boy, he really doesn't get it.

Toying with that cleric again?
If you play with monkeys, Master Raenef, you'll begin to devolve.
Monkeys?!
It's lunchtime, Master Raenef.
Okay.
......
Nothing. Shall we go?
What are you looking at, Eclipse?

파사

Are you finally sensing my presence, Eclipse?
Well, aren't you clever?
Hey, hey. Let's not go there. That's the maximum death magic.
Use that and you'll hit me--and half the woods.

I warned all of you not to interfere and yet you appear before my eyes. Why?
Yes, I heard your advisement through Meruhesae.
I've never been one for following orders.
Anyway, there's something I don't understand: no previous Raenef Demon Lord was ever interested in his heirs.
Have you developed a sentimental side?
Raenef Demon Lords routinely slaughter and replace their heirs.

Self-sacrifice isn't your style...
...but now you've abandoned revenge and ended your life earlier...
...In order to preserve the Raenef magic for your heir.
What are you up to?

...many years ago, you were placed under my care.

I remember...

You were a sharp kid, if rambunctious.
지저분
That little brat wrecked my study...
...and left it for me to clean up?!
Whatever could he have been thinking?
That little weasel.
쾅
......

If there was something that you wanted, you would use any means necessary to obtain it.
You were easy to manipulate.
What?!!
The reverie of recollection.
What is it that you want this time?

Fine. I had to ask.

I take my leave of you...

On one condition:

I beg you not to harm the red-headed swordswoman.

벌벌

Please...?

Now who has a sentimental side?

펑

I take my leave of you!!

Where am I?

You...
Don't know anything...
...about yourself.

Do you really believe that you are a true demon lord...
Raenef?
Who...?
That's my voice...?!
I detest...
...Everything about you.
I can't talk!!

Don't you think...
...a shell like you...
...it's about time for you to disappear?
For both our sakes...

...must
shatter!

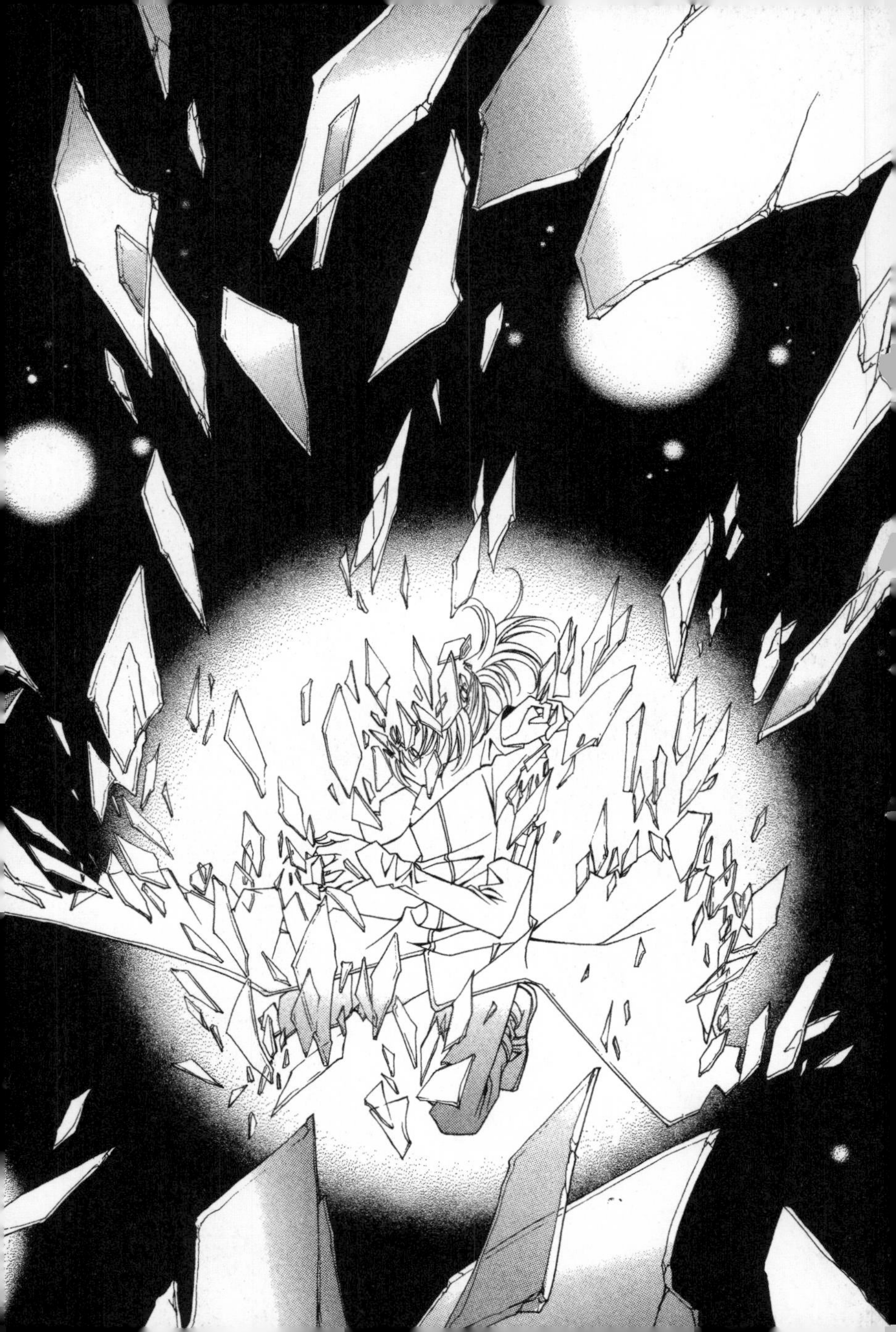

POW!
Noooooo!!!!
Huh?
콰당
빡
Don't worry, it's a special effect: ketchup.

Well...

...good morning to you too.

He's stronger than he looks.

I felt...
...Something... something really frightening.
I'm a Sword Master, A demon disaster, A pretty spell-caster, Come watch me now! la la la (lyrics by Erutis)
The light is thy voice, joy is thy gift...
Thine hands are the warmth of the world.
!

Am I hallucinating?

Hmm.

Hey-- Depraved Monk.
Why the sudden transformation into a real cleric?
!!

Shut up!! Who are you calling depraved?!!
You!

I am the heir to the High Cleric of Rased!!

You don't honestly think that your record is spotless, do you?
First, you used dark magic to summon a demon lord and now you live in his castle, mooching off of him. And that jewel on your cane--isn't that the emblem of Rased? You whack it about hither-dither, like it was some kind of costume jewel made out of paste! And to top it all off--
Help!
바둥 바둥
--you've befriended a demon lord!
결정타!
You're a depraved monk!
But, if the term offends you, I can always call you a phony.
오~
호호호호
확인 사살
푹

Aaack!
What?!
Ques... tion...
Fine!! Let go!
How dare you grab a young lady's leg?!!

I've been wondering about this for a while...

Hey, if you're trying to recover your dignity, give it up.

Erutis, you know a lot about clerics.

Eh?

...
I can't hear what you're saying!
Stop kidding around.
You know a lot about clerics, Erutis.
You're a Sword Master, Erutis.
How could you have been a mercenary?
I picked up things here and there.
I used to be a mercenary.

I'm amazed.

You were a mercenary?

It was nothing...

So, you threatened people, robbed and pillaged, and slept on the street?

Scoundrel(a)=Mercenary(b);
Erutis(c)=Mercenary(b);
therefore (a)=(c)

And, in the meantime, you were blinded by greed and sucked up to your leaders...

삼단 논법 성립

If you don't start using your head once in a while...
Then maybe I'll just knock it off!
You're already knocking it off.
Don't mistake mercenaries for villains!!

So why are you here?

Where did that question come from?

As I understand it...
...the only thing that keeps a mercenary in one place is money...
Money
¥
Mone
錢
₩
$
돈
...or some kind of profit.
What do you know about it?
You think that I'm that shallow?!
Friendship is another kind of commerce.
Isn't that a coin on the ground over there?
Where?
Pitter pat
......
Gasp.

Or maybe ...
...you're still here because of...
Some... one?
What...what are you talking about?!! Do you think that long dark hair and beautiful eyes are enough to--
Long dark hair?
Hyaah! I hope you get amnesia!

I want the demon lord, same as you.
오~호호호호
......
Supposedly, if you kill a demon lord, you gain special knowledge.
Did you call me?
You can't go sneaking up on people using transportation magic!
Owie!
......
You were planning on gaining knowledge from this guy?
As soon as I met him, I regretted it.

GaaaaSP!
I forgot--!!
What? What's the matter?
!!
I hadn't finished praying.
...
Oh, that's right. Today is the great day of prayer.

Great day of prayer?

Yes. As a demon lord, you wouldn't celebrate it.

Rased, rest in benevolent light upon thy temple. All light is thy glory.

150 years ago, during the Hangma War...

...the gods sacrificed themselves in order to save mankind.

Once a year, a day is set aside to pray for the souls of the dead gods and to thank them for their sacrifice.

All done. Let's play!

What do you wanna play, Raenef?

Just as I thought: prayer mode is an anomaly.

Now...

......

Huh?

!!

...the time approaches.

I heard something else...

......

What did you just say?

Chris's prayer mode is an anomaly?

Do you understand that curse, Eclipse?
Ha! Isn't it ironic, Eclipse...
That curse...

...that the Master of every incantation should be bound by one?

Are you speaking of the curse that the creatures of heaven cast upon you?

Well...you need no longer refer to it as a curse--it's more like a child's prank.

It is the insolence that bothers me.

Adapt myself to time...
Two days later, he died.
But, what he said to me that day...
...made me certain he had a plan.
He would not have died without some plan.

THE POWER THAT CONTROLS THE WORLD INFLUENCES ALL THINGS. EXISTENCE IS POSSIBLE ONLY WITHIN A GIVEN SPAN OF TIME.
THE ONE WHO CONTROLS TIME IS THE ONE WHO HAS THE WORLD IN HIS HANDS.

All things
exist within
time.

Rased, send forth thy light of wisdom to this temple.

Thine abundant wisdom and light shall be glorified forever.

This year's great day of prayer is a scorcher, is it not?

......

Well, this is the 150th year. Since this is the end of the 50th year for the third time, it stands to reason that extra warm energy is being emitted.

They say that humans forget their bitterness and pass into the Next World with the Third Passing Ceremony since their demise.
If that's true of humans, it may be true of gods. 50 years have passed three times for the gods, perhaps they will have forgotten their bitterness and gone on to the Spirit World.

Today is the gods' third 50th year since their sacrifice.
There is a curse tied to the name of Demon Lord Raenef.
A curse is created when the focus of mind and yearning collide. It is more powerful at the end of its life than at its birth.

The young demon lord will not be spared.
Chris...
...the god Rased will be with you.
The curse will commence soon.

Hm...
I never gave it much thought before...
...but it's a day of prayer for the gods who rid the world of the most ruthless demon lord during the Hangma War.
There's definitely a connection. Not just to the incident, but to our Raenef.
Hey!
What are you doing, Chris?
Erutis says that if you don't practice your sword fighting skills, she won't let you eat.
Be quiet!

I'm trying to solve a tremendously huge conspiracy right now!!
Threatening me with starvation-- that witch!!
What conspiracy?

Raenef, have you ever heard of the Third Passing Ceremony?
......

The celebration of a person's death for three years in a row?
Good job!

That's right. After the third year, a soul leaves all its bitterness in This World and moves on to the Next World.

What does the Third Passing Ceremony have to do with a conspiracy?

I believe it involves you.

Me?
My master told me that a curse is at the peak of its power at the end of its life, rather than at its birth.

And a demon lord's power begins at midnight, while a god's power begins at midday.
I think something interesting might happen today at noon.

!

Something interesting ?!!
...
What is it? Is it a surprise?
PANT! PANT!

That curse was meant for Raenef IV, but he's dead.

The curse never properly reached fruition.
I suspect the gods might appear before us, to attend to the matter.
Eh???

It should be interesting.

Are you sure you're a cleric?

Here's something else that's interesting.

Idiot? I've been easy on you because you're a girl.
Good to know your eyes aren't just decorations!
You guys are two sides of the same coin.
Don't you start!
...
I just felt as if someone was watching me...

Like a ripple on the ocean.
Soon...a wave will crest.
That's right.
How...
Is it possible?

They used time to their advantage.
They sacrificed their own lives in order to move the time connected to the name of Raenef.
I am a master of all incantations...
Including temporal incantations.
And thus, they were fools.
If I adjust time--even fractionally--their curse...

...comes
under my
control.
Time.
Is this what
you would
refer to as
"biding
one's time"?

Everything according to its time...
7

6
5
쏴아
4
하하..
3

!!
Master Raenef?

째깍

뎅뎅..

It's noon.

파아아

하아

This power...?

It is time.

화

아아

Who are they?!

What's happening?
The creatures of heaven!
They're so bright.
Is it noon already?
Creatures of heaven? Those are the gods?
The time has come. Child who holds the name of Raenef...
...your corporeal life will continue.
But the time has come for fulfillment of the curse placed upon your name.
What does that mean?

Lo, Demon Lord!!
Wait! STOP!!
What are you doing to Raenef?!
What is he talking about? I didn't do anything!!

The hour has come for your death!!!
!!
It is my time now.

Master Raenef?

파악

That power ...?

Creatures of heaven!!
Why are they here?
Master Raenef is in danger!!
Stop, Eclipse.
There is nothing you can do.
!!

The fulfillment has begun.
화아아아아
Until it is complete, there is nothing anyone can do.
!

As I see it, since the former Raenef is already dead, the curse should be ineffective.
I expected the gods to appear because they couldn't locate the soul of Raenef IV but--
That look...
That look...
That look is definitely...
Why does Raenef look like his evil twin from before?!!
Oh, calm down.

What are you staring at?
파아
Eclipse?
Or that young man with him?

Just as I thought.

That Raenef is the evil twin.

What are you doing?

No, he is not a false Raenef this time.
He is awakened.
He is far more complicated than his predecessor.
Wow...it didn't even faze him.
Who is that? He blocked Raenef's magic.

......

Hey, Eclipse! Does Raenef know that young man?

......

Hm. The atmosphere between those two is chilly.

He is the former Demon Lord Raenef.

Shut up!
It's like one of them owes the other a lot of money.
OOCH

Of course. The former Demon Lord Raenef.
YUP.
Uh huh.
Just as I thought.

What?!
What a dimwit.

Isn't he supposed to be dead?! Is that a ghost?
Don't ask me! I can only think for myself.
You said "just as I thought"-- what do you know?
I don't know any more than you do!
GRAB
You tease! You act like you know it all, but you don't have a clue.
What?! Did you just call me a tease?
Please.

I have enough to think about as it is. Please stop.
Er... sure thing.
best friends ♡
Fwoosh
You look as if you know what has happened to you.
I am not an idiot.

Master Raenef.

What is going on?
You died in my arms, Master Raenef.

Why are you so surprised, Eclipse?
Did you have so little faith in me as to believe I'd die from a simple curse?
......
At one point, I mentioned time.

How?

According to the curse, today was to have brought my death.

You died many years ago.
Are you saying that your death, years ago, was not due to the curse?

The curse...
...was tied to the name of Raenef.

!

It ingeniously manipulated time.
They shortened my life by 3,500 years and brought forth my son from the distant future to this time.
As such, my son was forced to exist in an unnatural time frame...
...where, ultimately, he would wipe himself out.
Your son from the distant future...
...is Raenef?
My head is spinning
Yes.
If you don't get it, take a nap.

I am a product of the future.
I was brought here through time. My personality was fragmented by the journey.
I obtained all of Raenef IV's magical abilities and intelligence...
While my innocent self arrived with only the magical powers within his body.
That is what the creatures of heaven were scheming for.

......
You understand.
For a demon, to lose his mind is to forfeit his existence.
If things proceed as planned, within a short span of time, you will die.
Because of the split, I will eventually go mad...
...and destroy myself.

However, magic is temporally unstable.
And, during the long span of time required for your heir to arrive, our magic will undoubtedly dissipate into space.
And from the distant, distant future, your heir will be drawn.
Ultimately, the Demon Lord Raenef will completely disappear from this world.

두근
I understand.
Disappear?
Raenef is going to disappear?
That's not what's important.
What did you mean, today was supposed to bring the hour of your death?

You are a servant of Rased...

...and a friend of Raenef, aren't you?

What's it to you?

What?
If you wish to save that child...
Use the power of your god to attack him.
END OF DEMON DIARY VOLUME 5

TOKYOPOP®

DEMON DIARY™

6

Art by Kara

Story by Lee Yun Hee

Preview for Volume 6

You Only Hurt The Demons You Love

Years ago, Chris was orphaned as a result of a demonic attack that decimated his entire village. The merciful god Rased saved Chris' life and buried Chris' memories of the devastation. Though Chris' memories were suppressed, his feelings of hatred toward demons remained...and only grew stronger with time.

With all of this in mind, you'd think it wouldn't be too hard to get Chris to attack a Demon Lord...and you'd be right! The evil Raenef V and Chris, successor to the High Cleric of the Temple of Rased, duke it out in a no-spells-barred magical melee!

DEMON DIARY

REALITY CHECK
REBIRTH
REBOUND
REMOTE June 2004
RISING STARS OF MANGA December 2003
SABER MARIONETTE J
SAILOR MOON
SAINT TAIL
SAIYUKI
SAMURAI DEEPER KYO
SAMURAI GIRL REAL BOUT HIGH SCHOOL
SCRYED
SGT. FROG March 2004
SHAOLIN SISTERS
SHIRAHIME-SYO: SNOW GODDESS TALES December 2004
SHUTTERBOX
SNOW DROP January 2004
SOKORA REFUGEES May 2004
SORCEROR HUNTERS
SUIKODEN May 2004
SUKI February 2004
THE CANDIDATE FOR GODDESS April 2004
THE DEMON ORORON April 2004
THE LEGEND OF CHUN HYANG
THE SKULL MAN
THE VISION OF ESCAFLOWNE
TOKYO MEW MEW
TREASURE CHESS March 2004
UNDER THE GLASS MOON
VAMPIRE GAME
WILD ACT
WISH
WORLD OF HARTZ
X-DAY
ZODIAC P.I.

NOVELS

KARMA CLUB APRIL 2004
SAILOR MOON

ART BOOKS

CARDCAPTOR SAKURA
MAGIC KNIGHT RAYEARTH
PEACH GIRL ART BOOK April 2004

ANIME GUIDES

COWBOY BEBOP ANIME GUIDES
GUNDAM TECHNICAL MANUALS
SAILOR MOON SCOUT GUIDES

CINE-MANGA™

CARDCAPTORS
FAIRLY ODD PARENTS MARCH 2004
FINDING NEMO
G.I. JOE SPY TROOPS
JACKIE CHAN ADVENTURES
KIM POSSIBLE
LIZZIE MCGUIRE
POWER RANGERS: NINJA STORM
SPONGEBOB SQUAREPANTS
SPY KIDS
SPY KIDS 3-D March 2004
THE ADVENTURES OF JIMMY NEUTRON: BOY GENIUS
TRANSFORMERS: ARMADA
TRANSFORMERS: ENERGON May 2004

TOKYOPOP KIDS

STRAY SHEEP

For more information visit www.TOKYOPOP.com

Mess with her...
Mess with her friend!
100% AUTHENTIC MANGA
T TEEN AGE 13+
www.TOKYOPOP.com